The Story of the ALPHABET

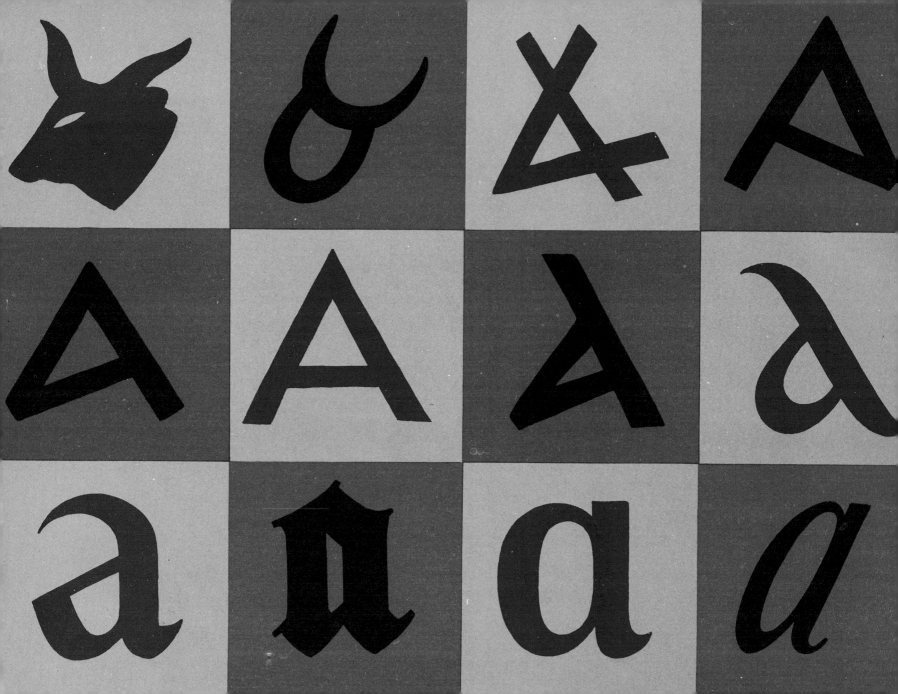

John R. Biggs

The Story of the ALPHABET

LONDON | OXFORD UNIVERSITY PRESS | 1968

Oxford University Press, Ely House, London W.1

Glasgow New York Toronto Melbourne Wellington Cape Town Salisbury
Ibadan Nairobi Lusaka Addis Ababa Bombay Calcutta Madras
Karachi Lahore Dacca Kuala Lumpur Hong Kong Tokyo

Printed in Great Britain at the Curwen Press,
Plaistow, London, E.13

Acknowledgements

The plates on pages 8, 10, 12, 13, 14, 15, 16, 17, 18, 19, 20, 22, 23,
24, 25, 26, 27, 29, 30, 31, 32, 33 and 35 are reproduced by kind permission of the Trustees of the British Museum.
 The author would also like to make grateful acknowledgement to the
Johnson Collection at Oxford for permission to reproduce the plates on
pages 38, 39, 40 and 41, and to Brighton College of Art for use of the
plates on pages 42, 43, 44, 45, 46 and 47.

THE STORY OF THE ALPHABET A short account of the development of the Roman (Latin) Alphabet

Every day, at the roadside, we see signs and symbols which give us warning of approaching hazards like level crossings, or hump bridges; that give us direction like 'straight ahead' or 'turn left', or inform us that a speed limit begins or ends. Similar pictorial signs were used to convey simple messages long before the shapes we know as letters of the alphabet were thought of.

But before we go any further let us be clear what we mean by an alphabet and then inquire how our own 'Latin' alphabet came into being and developed into the shapes we are familiar with and which you, the reader, are seeing now.

An alphabet is a series of symbols representing the sounds of speech. The signs in themselves do not mean anything—they represent the sounds of speech and only mean something when the letters are arranged in a particular order, that of words, which signifies speech. The

alphabet, then, is closely associated with speech—but it is evident that men could communicate with one another long before they had any way of recording their speech by means of writing, just as there are a number of primitive peoples existing today who talk to one another but cannot write or give any kind of permanence to their words.

Speech has the advantage of directness and the persuasive possibilities of tone of voice and gesture, but once the sounds of the voice have died away and the speaker has departed, only the fallible memory of the hearer is left of what was said. And of course it is impossible for a speaker to make himself heard in a far country (except by means of radio or television), or at any time but the present. But if the speaker's ideas are recorded in some form his ideas may influence people on the other side of the world and down many centuries.

People may thus speak to one another though they have never met and even when the speaker has long since died.

How did man learn to record his ideas so that his fellow men, and those who came after him, could benefit from his knowledge and experience? It is probable that long before man thought of associating shapes with the sounds made with his tongue and lips he used signs to give basic information, such as an arrow to indicate direction. We use such signs today, indeed, we are surrounded in our streets by signs and symbols which tell us what to do and what not to do, and which we disobey at our peril. In other words, we are today inventing and using signs, symbols and pictures in much the same way as primitive man thousands of years ago. That is why in this book we start with road signs that everybody sees and which everybody should understand. By analysing the thought

5

behind these signs we shall better understand the changes that have occurred in the development of the alphabet. The Highway Code gives us many examples of two of the main stages in the evolution of the alphabet, namely pictograms, or simplified pictures of the idea to be conveyed, and ideograms which are arbitrary shapes or signs which we learn to associate with the idea. Examples of pictograms are *level crossing with gate or barrier ahead; level crossing* without *gate or barrier ahead; hump bridge; services,* with a cup to represent cafeteria, and a knife and fork to signify restaurant facilities. There are many more. Examples of ideograms are the horizontal line

which means no entry, the diagonal line which indicates the end of the speed limit, and so on.

The object of all these is to convey an idea of one sort or another. Without a single word being used, warning or information is conveyed to our minds and we then act accordingly.

There is little doubt that long before man thought of using shapes to represent what was going on in his mind he used various devices to aid his memory, such as we do today when we tie a knot in a handkerchief to remind us to do something. Thus we might call the first stage in the evolution of the alphabet 'aids to memory' or *mnemonics*. A typical example is making notches in a stick to record the number of days that pass, or the number of cattle owned or sold. The Roman Catholic rosary is a similar aid to memory but which has also acquired strong religious associations for those who follow the Roman Catholic faith. In ancient Peru, a system of knots in cords of different thickness, length and colour became more than an aid to memory and a means of keeping numerical records, for by it simple news of recent events could be noted and official announcements made. These knotted cords are known as *quipus*.

The next important stage, and in which it is easy to see the ancestors of letters, is that of *picture-writing* or *pictograms*. Even today one of the simplest ways of conveying our meaning to someone whose language we do not know is to draw a picture of what we want to say. Where this is a simple, easily comprehended notion, as in the road signs, no difficulty arises. The meaning is easily understood and, also very important, should not be readily *mis*understood. Picture-writing was certainly a big step forward on the road to an efficient and simple means of recording ideas.

The limitations of any form of picture-writing are obvious. There is the difficulty of representing abstract ideas; only those things capable of being represented pictorially being possible. Nevertheless, even in picture-writing it is possible to extend the meaning of nouns into verbs. For example, if the simple shape of an eye represents the eye itself, by its position in relation to other signs, it could mean the act of seeing. A tear in the corner of the eye could mean weeping and, by association, sorrow or grief. So picture-writing is not so limited after all, even though it is far from being as efficient as an alphabet.

The Chinese and Japanese still use a form of writing in which most of the characters are derived from pictograms. A separate character is required for every word, therefore Chinese and Japanese have thousands of

different shapes to memorize whereas we have basically only twenty-six.

Once the idea was established that the words men spoke could be represented by shapes on a surface, it was only a matter of time and gradual change before an efficient alphabet was evolved. It is not surprising that more than one (indeed many) different sequences of shapes (alphabets) to represent language have been

devised in different places and at different times.

About five thousand years ago, in the region of the Rivers Tigris and Euphrates which was known as Babylon or Sumer, a system of writing was employed composed of wedge-shaped indentations in clay. This writing is called cuneiform. Writing was performed by means of a stylus made of wood or reed, cut at the end into a wedge shape, which was pressed into clay in sequences of patterns to form words. The clay was afterwards baked. These clay tablets, as they are often called, have proved very durable—at least they have survived the ravages of weather and damp, if not the breakages that pottery is heir to. In the beginning, cuneiform writing was used mainly for household and book-keeping accounts and noted only concrete words such as names of animals, plants and objects. Later the word signs were not only

used for the objects they depicted, but for their homonyms (that is, words having the same name but a different meaning), as if, in English, the picture of a bird's bill was used also for a commercial 'bill', the name 'Bill', and the syllable 'bil' in ability.

The cuneiform signs were at first a more or less realistic picture of the objects they stood for, but they gradually became simplified into purely conventional signs in which it is difficult to see the original shape. Although the cuneiform system of writing was unwieldy because of the great number of signs it required (six hundred to seven hundred) it was able to record the history of Babylon in considerable detail, so that we know more about life in Babylon than we do about life in our own country in some much more recent times.

An example of cuneiform is to be seen on page 17. Although for centuries cuneiform writing was the only international script and the great vehicle of civilization, the rise of Egypt and the decline of Babylon or Sumer saw the development of a form of writing in Egypt known as hieroglyphics. Strictly, the word meant 'priestly writings carved in stone', but the word has come to be applied not only to the carved signs incised in stone but to those written with a pen or brush.

The Egyptians used the hieroglyphic script for nearly 3,500 years, that is, from about 3100 B.C. until the reign of Diocletian, when the last known hieroglyphic inscription is dated A.D. 296. Later the Egyptians began to use a script, based on the Greek alphabet, known as Coptic and the knowledge of how to read and write hieroglyphics was lost until the 19th century.

The decipherment came about largely through the discovery in 1799 by soldiers in Napoleon's army at Rosetta of a slab of black basalt on which there were three inscriptions, the top one in hieroglyphics, the middle one in demotic, which is a cursive, or running form of hieroglyphics, and the bottom one in Greek, a language that was understood. It is known as the Rosetta Stone.

For over twenty years hieroglyphics still remained a mystery. Many people tried to solve it and made various guesses, some of which were later proved correct. By far the greatest contribution to the decipherment was that of a Frenchman, Jean François Champollion (1791–1831) who wrote a letter to the *Académie des Inscriptions* announcing his discovery and eighteen months later published a book, *Précis du système hiéroglyphique*, which laid the foundations for further decipherment and the growth of Egyptology.

The first clue to the decipherment was the observation that here and there a series of characters was surrounded by a line known as a cartouche which can be seen on page 11. It was assumed that the cartouche contained the name of a monarch, and on the Rosetta Stone the same cartouche is repeated six times with slight modifications and the Greek text suggested that the name was PTOLMEES or PTOLEMY. This gave the value of certain characters which could be used to help decipher other names, for example, CLEOPATRA. By checking and cross checking, assumptions were proved correct until finally the full meaning was revealed.

Pebbles with marks which resemble letters but are more likely to have magical or simply decorative significance than to be true ancestors of the alphabet.

It proved, however, that the Egyptians did not have an alphabet in the strict sense of the word which we have defined as a series of symbols representing the sounds of speech. About seven hundred signs were used, some of which were ideograms which indicated the meaning of a word pictorially without showing how it was to be read, and others were phonograms which indicated the consonants but not the vowels.

The hieroglyphics inscribed on temples, memorials and so on, are often very beautiful but the forms are too complex for easy writing by anybody not a professional scribe. A written version was developed known as hieratic which was still rather formal and used only for holy writings and other important documents. In turn a cursive script called demotic was evolved that was employed exclusively for secular purposes.

As we are primarily concerned with the Latin alphabet we must pass over quickly the stages about which scholars are not in full agreement. It is possible (indeed of some letters, probable) that the Phoenicians adapted

Egyptian characters for their own use. In turn, the early Greeks used the Phoenician alphabet as a basis for their own. What is quite certain is that the Greeks evolved an alphabet which was eventually modified by the Romans to become the alphabet we use today.

The word alphabet itself contains its history. The two parts of the word are *alpha* and *bet(a)*. *Alpha* is the first and *beta* is the second letter of the Greek alphabet. Just as we still refer to the alphabet as the ABC it has been a custom from very early times to arrange the letters in a particular order and to refer to the whole by the first two or three. Hence— the *alpha-beta* or alphabet.

But there is a possibility of the words being derived from the Egyptian and the shape of the letters themselves being simplified pictograms. The Egyptian word for ox was *aleph*. A capital A inverted (other letters have been turned round in the course of time) resembles an ox's head (see frontispiece) and by gradual modifications it may well have become our capital A.

It must be accepted that the Egyptian hieroglyph is the precursor of writing in the West.

We have been talking about letters being modified in shape and it will help in our understanding of the various versions of familiar letters if we consider what are the influences or conditions which tend to modify or change the shapes of letters. First among the influences we must place that of the *tool or instrument* with which a letter is made. Assuming that the general shape of a letter is known (say the triangular form of capital A) the shape created by a chisel-edged pen will be different from that made with a brush or a graver. Second we might place the *material* the letters are made in or on. It is evident that letters made on a smooth vellum will tend to be different from those cast in bronze or concrete or made of neon-lighting tube. Third, the *speed* with which a letter is made will tend to alter its shape, as we shall see later. Fourth is the influence of *fashion* or the custom of the age—it is natural for every age to want to make things in a way which will reflect the spirit of the time. Fifth is the *purpose* for which the letter is made—we would not expect the greengrocer or the fishmonger to fashion his letters setting out the current day's prices with the same care and dignity we would demand of a sculptor on a memorial to a Prime Minister or on the façade of a city hall, both of which may survive for centuries. Sixth, we cannot rule out the influence of the *personality* of the scribe or letterer, but in this context such an influence is likely to be slight Individual scribes have little or no major influence on the shape of letters— I mean in the sense that a scribe does not invent his own alphabet (otherwise he would be the only one to understand it). He accepts the forms current in his age and makes such minor modifications as he feels fitting and which will be legible and comprehensible to his contemporaries.

All these influences are operative in some degree, at all times. Sometimes one influence will be dominant and another time another of the influences will predominate.

Under 'custom of the age' we must include direction of writing, that is, whether from right to left or left to right. (We will not consider Chinese or Japanese which is written in vertical columns from top to bottom). We accept today that writing, and, of course, printing and other forms of lettering, read from left to right. But it was not always so. Egyptian demotic, and hieratic script read from right to left. Semitic script from the beginning down to modern Hebrew and Arabic has always been from right to left. Ancient Greek script was written in the same direction as was the early writing in Italy, but for some reason not fully explained it gradually became the custom to write from left to right.

There was an intermediate stage when writing went alternately from left to right and then on the next line from right to left, and so on. Indeed, the earliest known Roman inscription in stone on the Lapis Niger, 5th century B.C., has its lettering reading to and fro on alternate lines. This alternating of direction of writing was known by the Greeks as *boustrophedon* because of its resemblance to the direction of ploughing in the fields.

The earliest known Latin inscription is that on a fibula or metal buckle known as the Praeneste Fibula (about

7th century B.C.). Here the writing runs from right to left. It will be noticed that the letter E has its horizontal bars on the left of the vertical instead of on the right because this is the easiest and most natural way of making the letter E if the hand is moving from right to left. In *boustrophedon* script we find letters like E pointing to right or left on alternate lines according to the direction in which the line was made. Notice also that the letters have no serifs (the little horizontal finishing strokes at the end of the stems of typical classical Roman letters). There is little or no space between words.

We have already said that the Latin alphabet is derived from the Greek, indeed, many of the letters are exactly the same. Another alphabet still widely used is the Cyrillic which is also derived from the Greek and is used for the Russian and Bulgarian languages.

But we are concerned with the Latin alphabet and the changes that have taken place in its form since the Praeneste Fibula.

As Rome's military prowess extended so did her skill in engineering and the utilitarian crafts, not least in lettering. By the 2nd century A.D. a form of capital letter had been evolved which may have been equalled but never surpassed for both legibility and beauty. Because so much of the lettering was cut in durable stone much of it has survived. Because Roman craftsmen went with the armies to carve milestones, memorials, altars to their gods, and inscriptions on public buildings of many kinds, good Roman lettering is to be found wherever the Romans occupied the territory for any length of time. (It should be mentioned in passing that they also left a lot of indifferent and shoddy lettering even though its antiquity may claim our interest. I think we should always distinguish between historic and aesthetic merit or interest— the two do not necessarily go together.)

Probably the most famous Roman inscription is that on the base of Trajan's Column in Rome which was erected about A.D. 114. It deserves its fame, because its letters have a clarity, legibility and elegance which are an inspiration to all who are interested in the art of lettering, but it should not blind us to the beauty of many

other inscriptions equally as good. With that in mind I have chosen as an example of classical Roman incised lettering the inscription from the Forum of Viroconium, the Roman city at Wroxeter just outside Shrewsbury. The tablet is now in the Rowley's House Museum in Shrewsbury. It is 12 feet by 4 feet and like the Trajan inscription and many other similar inscriptions, the size of the letters is largest for the top line and diminishes slightly on each successive line. The proportions of some of the letters differ slightly from Trajan but are equally good in their context. The N is narrower than Trajan as are the capital T and C. The R has a smaller bowl and longer tail than Trajan. There is less space between the lines than Trajan but the whole effect is a clean, crisp texture presenting a generally magnificent and imposing appearance. The inscription records the construction of the building in honour of the Emperor Hadrian in A.D. 130.

Before we go any further let us consider the tools and materials that had been used in Egypt, Greece and Rome, and in more primitive communities.

Marks resembling letters on pebbles and stones made with fingers in coloured earths and other staining or colouring materials are to be seen from very early times, but it is doubtful whether they can be considered letters. They may have had some magical or other symbolic significance but cannot be regarded as true writing.

Pieces of wood and pottery (potsherds) have been used for writing on for thousands of years. In the British Museum is to be seen a wooden panel with writing on used by the Egyptians as a model for pupils to copy. The material used by pupils for their exercises was usually fragments of pottery or stone called *ostraca*. Fragments still exist showing how the student had practised the same letter over and over again. The tool used was a kind of brush or pen made of a thin reed frayed at the end to soften it and retain ink. A box of pens is shown on page 12.

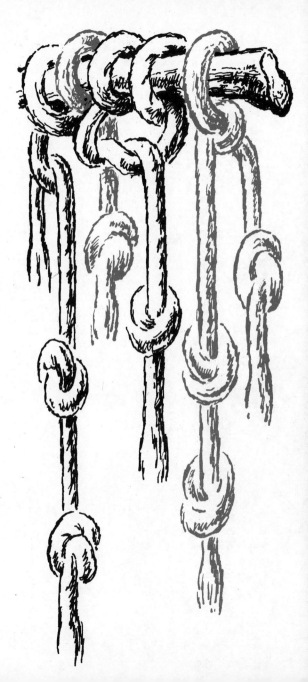

'Quipu' or knot writing. A primitive method of conveying simple messages said to be still employed by isolated shepherds in such parts as Peru. More of an aid to memory than true writing.

It is not always easy to be sure what ink was used for a particular example but early authors refer to the use of the liquid of the cuttle-fish, soot and gum, and gall apples.

The chief writing material for documents of all kinds in ancient Egypt was papyrus, a name which gives us our word paper. Papyrus was a reed which grew by the Nile. The stems were cut into thin strips and laid on a board, each strip slightly overlapping its neighbour. At right-angles to this layer other strips of papyrus were laid and pressed together before being allowed to dry in the sun. As sheets were made by overlapping strips it was possible to continue almost indefinitely. As papyrus is brittle and tends to crack if folded, it was rolled on a stick at each end. The columns of writing were at right-angles to the long side. Scrolls are known over one hundred feet long. The Greeks used papyrus as well as the Egyptians. Their word for papyrus was *biblos* and the word came to be used for a book. It is from this word *biblos* that the word Bible is derived. The Latin peoples used the word *liber* for book which gives us our word library. The roll form of book was called the *volumen* which name lingers on in our word volume. It is probable that a book or volume was originally a convenient sized roll and poems and other literary works were thus divided into 'books'. When scrolls were stored on shelves a vellum label called a *titulus* was attached for identification. This is the origin of the word title. So you see that many words we commonly use have their origin in the history of writing.

Another material used was vellum or parchment which is the skin of sheep and goats treated in such a way as to make writing on both sides easy. It is a beautiful material to write on with a quill pen and it endured as the chief writing material until long after the invention of printing about 1440.

Vellum has always been a comparatively rare and there-

The Rosetta Stone. A black basalt block inscribed with characters in three languages, Egyptian Hieroglyphics, Hieratic and Greek. This inscription was the key to understanding hieroglyphics.

fore expensive material and so was only used for important documents. For everyday ephemeral jottings a wax tablet was used by the Egyptians and then by the Romans, and it eventually had an influence on the shape of the letters. A wax tablet, illustrated on page 18, is usually a small panel of wood in which is a shallow depression to contain wax. They were often fastened together by rings to form a kind of book.

Writing on the wax was made with a pointed piece of wood, bone, ivory, bronze or other metal according to the wealth and status of the owner. It was known as a stylus. One end, for writing, was pointed and the other end flattened for use as an eraser by smoothing the wax after writing had been scratched in it.

When you consider the nature of this material—smooth and slippery—and the stylus a mere pointed stick, it is evident that the refinements of form possible to the carver cutting letters in marble would be quite impossible.

It must be borne in mind when considering the nature of a particular script or letter that from very early times there were usually two or three different scripts in use at the same period, each style being appropriate for its intended purpose. A careful, imposing or ostentatious style was employed for important writing such as holy books, royal documents and so on, which reflected the esteem with which the august nature of the message was regarded. For personal letter-writing, notes and trivial jottings, a cursive form was used which might seem very different from the more dignified 'literary' form as most people's ordinary handwriting differs from type which is the kind of letter form most often read today. There was also frequently an intermediate 'hand' for business and legal documents, not so imposing as the religious or regal writing, but clearer and more dignified than the vernacular cursive hand.

The cartouche of Ptolemy and Cleopatra which gave clues to the meaning of some of the hieroglyphics and led to the decipherment of the remainder.

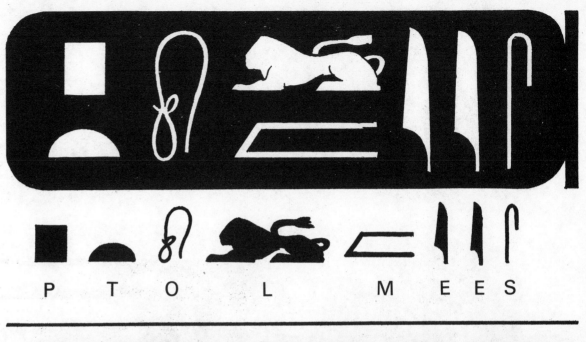

P T O L M E E S

K L E O P A T R A

Generally speaking, the cursive and commercial writing was a less careful (or even debased) form of the 'literary' style, but forms also evolved under the influence of speed which eventually were refined by skilled practitioners into admirable styles.

If we ask ourselves what is most likely to be the prime influence on writing in any given period the answer is probably that letter form which is most often seen. We may also say, or wish, that the best is always the strongest influence and that the less good is only the result of lesser skill. This is clearly not always so but these ideas will, I think, help our understanding of the forms and changes in shape that occurred over the centuries.

It may be said that in every age there is a norm of letter form which is accepted, whether consciously or unconsciously, as normal and departures from this norm are recognized as being in some way special. That being so, it may be said that the norm, the dominating influence in Roman times, was the inscriptional, classical letter cut in stone and readily seen on public buildings without the competition with shop fronts, traffic signs and so on, such as we see today. So if a Roman thought of the perfect normal letter, it would most likely be letters such as we see in the Wroxeter inscription, or on the Trajan Column.

These inscriptional forms then were a dominating influence in the development of writing and the alphabet (or alphabets) as we know it, but it is possible that the more cursive forms employed when writing on wax tablets and papyrus had a greater influence on scribes than has generally been admitted.

A potsherd showing a student's exercise in forming letters correctly.

An Egyptian pen or brush case.

Two examples of the more cursive Egyptian writing which was developed from hieroglyphics. The illustration on the left shows the instruction of King Amenemhet, on the right a charm for dispelling headaches.

The Wroxeter inscription and thousands of other similar items are in a form of letter very aptly suited to the material and purpose. The letters are cut in a V section into the stone and the serifs at the end of the strokes are a neat and efficient way of bringing the chisel to the surface and finishing off the stems. It is obviously possible to make stems without serifs but it is a natural gesture to carry the horizontal at the end beyond the vertical of the stem, which is slightly rounded as it comes up from the depth of the V, as it joins the horizontal at the surface. It is a matter of the artist-craftsman's feeling how big the serif is and the degree of its curvature. Though the serif may be regarded as a decorative feature it may also be considered functional, emphasizing as it does the horizontal, the direction of reading, besides being a natural outcome of the material and tools and their method of use.

One of the characteristics of these classical letters, which, it will be noticed, are capitals only, is that some of the strokes are thicker than others and that the thicknesses and thinnesses occur in a systematic way. It is believed, largely on this evidence, that most of the famous inscriptions were just 'written' with a flat brush which, held in the right hand in the usual way, would produce thicks and thins naturally according to the direction the stroke was made in. Certainly, there is no purely practical reason why strokes incised in stone should differ in thickness. Early inscriptions were both sans serif and monotone, that is, all strokes approximately the same thickness. After being 'written' by a scribe or lettering artist it is suggested that another craftsman cut the letters in stone. This is likely for the most important inscriptions, but many of the lesser memorials, tombstones and mile-posts look as

though scarcely any preliminary sketch had taken place so careless is the spacing and form of the letters, which crowd towards the end of lines and even run off the edge.

With the introduction of the chisel-edged quill pen, scribes tried to render the form and proportion of the inscriptional capitals with an instrument ill adapted to the task and what are known as square caps or Quadrata are the result. Such letters could not be written quickly with a chisel-edged pen and though in the hand of a skilful scribe square caps are beautiful, nevertheless they cannot be regarded as true pen forms.

One cannot expect an intelligent penman to write for long without forms emerging that are more natural to the tool, and in time, another style of capitals known as Rustic was developed. You will see these illustrated on page 22 and it is evident that these are true pen forms—

14

the thicks and thins are as they would come if a pen was held in the usual way and written at a moderate speed.

The thinness of the vertical strokes shows that the pen was held with its edge at an oblique angle with the writing line, resulting in thinnish verticals and thickish horizontals which gives what is to us an unconventional feeling, particularly in letters like E and F. It is a very 'condensed' letter, that is, all the letters are narrower than normal. There is usually little or no space between words and only very rudimentary punctuation.

The Rustic style became sufficiently popular to start influencing the inscription cutters and we find stones on which the main lines are in Rustic (really a pen letter) which in a sense is as illogical as for the scribes to imitate inscriptional letters. The rise of Rustic with inscriptional and later with cursive forms declined but was revived hundreds of years later after a period of disuse. As time went on, the pen became the norm or dominating influence and it is then that the inspiration of informal Roman writing seems to have played a part.

Informal cursive hands have a tendency for letters to be irregular in height, for some letters to project above and some to go below the normal height. In the first place these projections would not be conscious or deliberate, but a result of speed and lack of care in the physical act of writing. But by degrees these ascenders and descenders, as we call them, became an accepted element and led the way to what we now call lower-case or 'small' letters.

The term lower-case is one derived from printing, in which craft it was the custom to put types in two cases, one of them tilted above the other. Capital letters were kept in the upper case, and the small letters related to them in the lower case—hence the term lower-case. A better term, at least when referring to written letters, is minuscule for small letters; its companion term is majuscule, meaning large letters or capitals.

We shall now see the gradual evolution of minuscule letters from majuscules. The chief tool was the chisel-edged quill pen, the quills being obtained from geese or turkeys for the larger writing, down to quills from the thrush for very small writing. The shape of letters, particularly the position of the thick strokes and the thickest

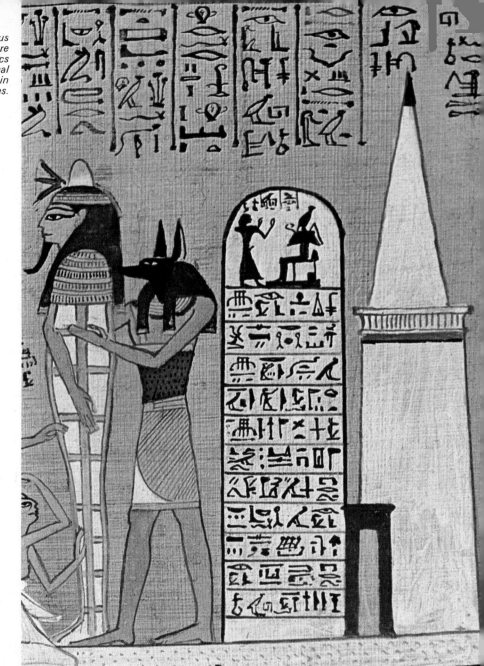

A page from a famous Book of the Dead. Here we see hieroglyphics written in vertical columns as well as in horizontal lines.

A stone relief showing scribes recording. One writes in cuneiform with a stylus on a waxed board, the other writes Aramaic on a scroll with a pen.

parts of curved letters, is conditioned by the angle at which the edge of the pen is held in relation to the writing line. If the edge is parallel to the writing line, horizontal strokes will be the minimum possible and verticals the maximum possible thickness. If held at forty-five degrees both verticals and horizontals will be of medium thickness and the greatest thickness of stroke will be those going from top left to bottom right. Only a few degrees difference in angle alters the character of the letter considerably, as a close study of examples will make obvious.

Let us remember when talking about influences, changes of style and form that they occurred over long periods of time. One style does not end abruptly and another begin overnight. After a new style has begun the old may persist even after centuries. Styles in art and design are rarely sharply defined and often no useful purpose is served by trying to assert that a particular style began at a precise date. What is more reasonable is to say that a particular style was fully fledged at a given period while being aware that examples of a different style might be found to be contemporary with it.

The style that is usually regarded as following Rustic is that called 'uncial'. Uncial letters might be thought of as rounded square caps. They are basically capitals, though rudimentary ascenders and descenders are present. Some letters like M and D are more rounded than in square caps, and the abundance of curves gives a general effect which is rich, stately and opulent.

As early as the 3rd century B.C. men wrote in a hand which is nearer to uncial than any other recognized style, and by the 1st century B.C. in the oration of Hyperides for Lycophron we have a free, elegant, highly accomplished writing which must be called uncial because of its rounded quality. The writing was on papyrus.

It is not uncommon that when a style of writing (or of art or decoration) is fully formed it is followed by slow decline or decadence. But over the centuries uncial writing improved and this improvement may be attributed to the change of material from papyrus to vellum which is a much more kindly, sympathetic writing surface and gave greater scope to the scribe for exercising his skill as a calligrapher.

16

*Cuneiform writing.
List of five fields
with their dimensions.
About 1980 B.C.*

An Egyptian wax tablet in diptych (two leaf) or codex form.

An enlargement of some of the writing still visible on the wax after almost 2000 years.

The Praeneste Fibula—the oldest known Latin inscription.

18

Greek capitals incised in stone. These are crisply cut and clearly seen as the ancestor of our own alphabet.

The Wroxeter inscription. One of the finest examples of classical Roman incised capitals now in Rowley's House Museum, Shrewsbury.

21

(a) *Quadrata or square caps. A penman's laboured version of inscriptional capitals.*

(b) *Rustic Capitals—a true pen form. Eventually influenced the inscription cutters who copied it in stone.*

We have said that the most practical shape for a book made of papyrus was a scroll, but vellum being made of the skin of sheep or goats is limited in size by the size of sheep and goats. The natural thing is to fold the rectangular sheet of a whole prepared skin, which makes two leaves or four pages. These folded sheets may then be grouped and sewn together at the fold. The result is the rectangular-prism shape which we normally associate with books. A book in this form rather than a scroll, is called a codex (plural codices).

There are a number of very famous codices in the British Museum, perhaps one of the greatest is the Codex Sinaiticus, so called because it was discovered in a monastery on Mount Sinai. It is a Bible. The New Testament is complete but the Old Testament has a number of books missing. The page is almost square with usually four columns of some of the finest Greek uncials in the world. In contrast to some of the later Bibles we shall be noting, there is a complete absence of decoration—the imposing effect being the result of carefully proportioned margins with just the right size of letter and length of line and space between lines. These factors, size, weight of letter, space and so on, are very important and greatly affect the appearance of lettering and are, in a sense, inseparable from the study of the alphabet.

It is not certain how early uncials were used for Latin but it was definitely employed as a literary hand as early as the 4th century A.D. There are many fine early MSS. written in uncials which is a style that has recently increased in popularity among modern scribes and letterers. Victor Hammer has designed, and typefounders have produced, a 20th-century uncial type which is beautiful if limited in its application today.

The word uncial was first used by St. Jerome and signified literally 'an inch high'—but probably it really meant 'large letters'. Between the 5th and the 8th centuries, at the same time as the uncial letter was widely practised, a more easily written book-hand with obvious ascenders and descenders was developed and called half-uncial. Again, the word uncial as pertaining to an inch is irrelevant, and it is further misleading because it seems to imply that half-uncial grew out of uncial. The general character of half-uncial is largely minuscule whereas uncial is nearer to capitals. It is more likely that the dominant influence was the Roman cursive rather than the formal uncial, though of course the two styles have some common characteristics. As half-uncial has a greater number of letters with ascenders and descenders we can begin to see the ancestor of our own small letters or lower-case emerging.

With the decline of the power of Rome and the rise in importance of Christianity with its monasteries and scriptoria (places where writing was done) local tastes had a chance to flourish and so national hands were evolved from the original Roman cursive. The national style that was developed in Spain was called Visigothic; in South Italy it was called Lombardic or Beneventan, and in

(c) *Uncial writing. A true and noble pen form. These 'large' letters are known as majuscules but already some letters are beginning to extend above and below the line.*

(d) *Half-Uncials. Rather misnamed as half-uncials; are more a development of Roman Cursive than the more formal uncials. Ascenders and descenders fully established.*

France the script was given the name of Merovingian. Other countries, too, developed subtly national characteristics and in Ireland and England a style was developed and practised with such superb mastery and authority that certain examples of it can be included among the world's great masterpieces of art and calligraphy. The two greatest are the *Book of Kells,* and the *Lindisfarne Gospels.*

The *Lindisfarne Gospels* (also known as the 'Durham Book') are said to have been written by Eadfrith, Bishop of Lindisfarne, a small island off the coast of Northumberland near the Scottish border, which became a great centre of English writing. The text is in what is often called the Irish or Anglo-Saxon half-uncial, a magnificent hand, strong, bold, and decorative. It is written with a straight pen, that is, with the edge of the pen parallel to the writing line so that verticals are thick and horizontals are thin. There are chunky, triangular serifs at the top of stems, and the space between lines is about twice the height of the letter.

The Lindisfarne Gospels. A major masterpiece. The text is written in half-uncials known as Irish, or Insular, or Anglo-Saxon half-uncials.

Beatus Page from the Evesham Psalter. English, about A.D. 1250-60.

The *Book of Kells*, so called because of its association with the monastery of Kells, was not, for certain, written there. Recent scholarship suggests that it was begun at Iona and 'there is a possibility that all the work was done there'. This splendid volume is very similar to the *Lindisfarne Gospels* and is another major masterpiece. It is notable for the fantastic initials that writhe with vitality and are filled with swirling scrolls and inextricable interlacements and magical colour. These two volumes must be seen to be believed; at the time of writing, the *Book of Kells* is in Dublin, and the *Lindisfarne Gospels* are on view at the British Museum.

The next great period in the history of the Latin script is the age of Charlemagne.

The revival of learning brought with it a desire to reform the handwriting through which the literary or religious works were made manifest. In 789 a decree called for a revision of church books. It must be remembered that one of the ways of speeding up the making of books was for a number of scribes to be in a room (scriptorium) and to write while one person dictated. It is obvious that errors would be likely to occur owing to mishearing or ordinary human fatigue. Moreover, scribes were individuals, and unlikely all to make the same errors. Of the copies produced, there was no certainty that all would be the same. If these volumes were distributed and in turn used as copies, it is easy to see that by degrees errors would increase, and a need for revision and going back to the original would arise.

Charlemagne invited Alcuin, a scholar from York, England, to undertake the revision of texts. Alcuin was made Abbot of St. Martin's at Tours, France, from 796–804, and under him a style of clear legible minuscules was created that became a standard for the many new versions of the Vulgate Bible which were required. This script, known as the Caroline (Carolingian, Carlovingian) minuscule, might be regarded as the direct ancestor of the letters you are reading now. It is the prototype of modern lower-case as we know it, though a minuscule style can

24

The evolution of a few letters from majuscule to miniscule.

clearly be seen emerging in Roman cursive script. Ascenders and descenders are fully established and integrated harmoniously with the large letters and with one another. Large letters are sometimes uncial or half-uncial, sometimes Rustic, and sometimes based on square caps. The space between lines is almost three times the height of the letters (disregarding ascenders and descenders) which makes for clarity and legibility.

Such a practical, speedy and beautiful script brought prestige to the scriptorium at Tours and its influence soon spread throughout Europe. Indeed it might be regarded as the basic hand of Europe until the various local influences and the pressure of speed and the need to save space brought about a narrowing of the letters and consequent blackening of the page, which culminated in 'Gothic' script. The word Gothic is not altogether satisfactory,

Benedictional of St. Ethelwold 10th century A.D. A magnificent example of English writing and illuminating.

25

(a) *Roman Cursive. The deed of sale of a slave written on papyrus A.D. . . . . This is a free but clear legible hand and it is not difficult to see how this kind of writing led to the miniscule which is the parent of our lower-case.*

(b) *Caroline Miniscule. About A.D. 800. This is the direct ancestor of the lower-case type in which most books are now printed.*

26

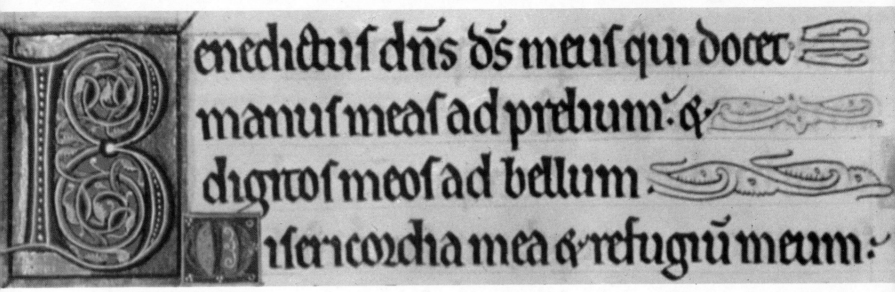

enedictus dns ds meus qui docet

manus meas ad prelium. &

digitos meos ad bellum.

misericordia mea & refugiu meum:

(a) 13th-century black letter. Rich and decorative but to our eyes not very legible.

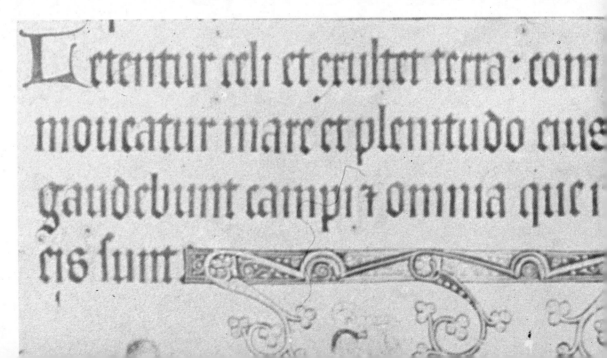

Letentur celi et erultet terra: com

moueatur mare et plenitudo eius

gaudebunt campi et omnia que

eis sunt

(b) 14th-century black letter.

Part of an inscription engraved in bronze on a tombstone in Marburg. 1481. The lettering is 'black letter', which is basically a pen form.

(a) Initial L from 'Le Livre de Matheolus', Lyon, 1492. The letter itself is calligraphic and the whole is cut on wood from which it was printed.

(b) Enlargement of a few lines of the Gutenberg 42-line Bible.

though it will be familiar to the general reader as applied to a style of church architecture. The term was used by Italian humanists in a pejorative or derisory sense to express their disapproval of the style of architecture and art which seemed to contradict all the canons of their beloved classic philosophy of art. They regarded the exuberance and the homeliness to be found in soaring steeples and carved façades and misericords as barbarous compared with the simplicity and serenity of classic art and dubbed it 'Gothic' because they associated barbaric tastes with the Goths. Today we associate the word Gothic with a glorious period in our history—the Middle Ages. A more satisfactory description might be medieval as the style flourished during that era.

Another more descriptive and better term is used for this script—black letter. Certainly, a compact page of this is very black when compared with a page of Caroline minuscules and therefore the word has much to recommend it, despite certain ambiguities. This black, angular,

condensed script was also called 'text' or textura, particularly when the style was crystallized in type.

The tendency for the letters to become condensed and angular had started about the time William the Conqueror came to England (1066) and during the succeeding four centuries letters became extremely narrow, angular and, to our eyes, very illegible until in the 15th century there was another renaissance, reformation, indeed revolution, in the art of calligraphy.

The 12th, 13th, 14th and 15th centuries saw not only the development of those rich dark scripts but the prosperity of the illuminator. It was an age of faith when men believed they were working to the glory of God and produced splendid monuments to their own talent and skill. The scribe who wrote the text would rarely illustrate or illuminate the the initials or otherwise decorate the pages. A different kind of person and temperament is required for the discipline to the point of monotony that writing a long text demands, from the rich imagination

and sensitive draughtsmanship required of an illustrator. Black letter reached its best in the 12th and 13th centuries, after that, there was a gradual decline.

It is well known that most of the writing and illuminating was done in monasteries and other religious houses, but far from all was done by monks. Secular scribes and artists were employed by the monasteries. They lived in the religious community while they worked but when the job was done many moved on to look for work in other monastic establishments or wherever patronage was available. So it is not surprising to find a particular artist's style cropping up in books made in different places.

I suppose the typical Gothic or black letter is that shown in the illustration on page 27. It will be seen that the letter i is a straight stem with a kind of diamond shape at the head and foot. A letter u is composed of two of these side by side—but so is an n; letter m is three of these strokes—but so is a w. There is only the minutest line connecting at the top or bottom to distinguish between

the letters so that many words are practically illegible. Imagine the word minimum! Not the kind of letter for books or magazines to be read in buses or trains...

Nevertheless, the various forms of black letter can be extremely beautiful. Not all are as condensed and angular as our example which is composed almost entirely of straight lines. Some have a number of curves in letters like a, s and g, and have earned the name Rotunda.

When we come to the 15th century the intellectual eruption of the Renaissance, and the weakening of religious influence which was one of the consequences of classical humanism, together with the invention of printing from movable types, created all the conditions for a major reformation of writing or rather its transformation into printing.

For over a thousand years the chisel-edged pen had been the dominating influence. When inscriptions were cut in stone on tombs, the letter was black letter—a pen-man's letter. When a legend was engraved on a brass memorial, the model followed by the engraver was black letter. It was the pen which pointed the way that letters should be made. But the quill was to meet a formidable rival in the graver and file of the punch-cutter who produced the means of making types and could produce thousands upon thousands of identical letters.

The invention of printing from movable types was an important event not only in the history of the alphabet but in the history of civilization. The ability to reproduce thousands of copies of a manuscript in a short time not only opened up the possibility of universal literacy but made the rapid spread of knowledge a reality. When a printer could produce 'as many words in a day as a scribe could in a year' it is evident that, very rapidly, knowledge could be amassed and made available wherever books could be carried. Never before in history had such an expansion of learning and culture been possible and in such a short space of time. We can say that the invention of printing from movable types changed the world. Our culture is conditioned by print.

The credit for the invention of printing from movable types is usually given to Johann Gutenberg of Mainz in Germany, about 1440. Centenaries and other official celebrations are based on that date. He did not invent printing as such, because the printing of playing-cards and devotional prints from wood-blocks had been an established trade in Europe for about fifty years and a million prints had been made from woodcuts in Japan as early as A.D. 770.

Most of the crafts involved in the manufacture of type and printing such as engraving, casting in lead, paper making, making of presses for printing, were already in existence when Gutenberg came along. He combined the skills and made some of them more precise than ever before so that a new industry was created.

'Movable types' means that every letter of the alphabet and every punctuation mark was cast in metal (mainly lead) with the letter projecting at the top of a small rectangular prism called the body of the type. It was necessary for the body of every letter to be the same height so that when the letters were set they would line up properly. When a given text had been set and printed, the letters could be distributed to their allotted compartment in a tray called a case, and then reset for another job.

It meant that once the type was set up, a very large number of copies could be taken in a comparatively short space of time, though, of course, Gutenberg was slow compared with modern printing. Another advantage, besides speed, was the ability to make corrections. Mistakes could easily be rectified at the proof stage. Once corrected, it was then sure that every copy would be the same—never a certainty in the days of the manuscript. A scholar in England reading a given book could be sure he was reading exactly the same text as a scholar in France, Italy, Germany or anywhere else in the world reading a book of the same edition.

The prime impulse of the early printers was not so much aesthetic as scholarly or commercial—by that I mean their object was to multiply manuscripts so much more rapidly than scribes could do and so facilitate the spread of learning. As a model of letter form was necessary in order to fashion their types it was natural that they should take the normal book-hand of their day and country. Their aim, at first, was to produce books which resembled the hand-written manuscripts as closely as possible and to the untrained eye many early printed books might at first or even second glance be mistaken for manuscripts. Among some book lovers a certain amount of aesthetic snobbery prevailed—the Duke of Urbino refused to have a printed book in his library. A parallel prejudice occurs in our own day when some people still believe that hand-made objects are necessarily better than mechanically produced ones. This is not so. Every machine is a tool and every tool a machine, however simple it may be. A machine is but an extension of man.

As Gutenberg lived in Germany the hand he used on which to model his type was that current in his own locality round the junction of the Rivers Rhine and Main. It was a compact, black letter, typically German. The illustration

30

on page 27 shows what a magnificent page was produced—but remember that the text only was printed;
the decoration was added by hand by the illuminators or
rubricators as they came to be called. The scribe's craft,
like that of the illuminator, was clearly doomed; but for a
generation or so, those that remained could contribute
to their living by embellishing printed books, where space
was often left for the rubricator's art.

Before leaving Gutenberg it is necessary to make one
or two things clear. Although it is now generally accepted
that Johann Gutenberg of Mainz was the first man to
make printing from movable types a practical proposition
and to establish a business to be passed on from generation to generation, much of the evidence is indirect. There
is no piece of printing with Gutenberg's name on it, nor
do any of the books attributed to him specifically say he
printed them.

The most important of the books attributed to him is
the Mazarin or forty-two line Bible, so called because each
page has forty-two lines per column. This is undoubtedly
one of the most distinguished books ever produced. But
the date of production has been deduced from the colo-
phon in which the rubricator records that he finished his
work on 24 August 1456. Scholars now agree that it was
printed between 1453 and 1455, sixteen years after the
lawsuit against him in 1439 which proved that he was
even then working on a printing process.

Gutenberg's press was taken over by Fust and
Schöffer who produced the magnificent Latin Psalter,
a part of which is reproduced on this page.

From now on the pen will have a diminishing, though
by no means negligible, influence on the shapes of the
letters of the alphabet. Printing types will show more
and more the effect of the manufacture of type by means
of punches and moulds.

In order to understand these forms it will be necessary
to give an outline of how type is made.

Type is cast from a mould, which, in principle, is the
same as the familiar domestic jelly mould, but it has to
be made much more accurately. The problem, then, is to
manufacture the moulds which must be small for making
type like you are reading now, precise in form, and the

31

The noble Psalter produced by the successors to Gutenberg's business, Fust and Schoeffer. The first two-colour printing.

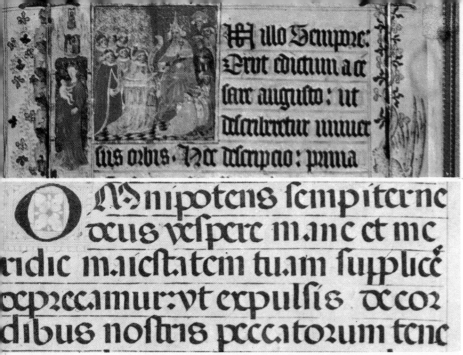

(a) The Lovel Lectionary (before A.D. 1400). Typical Gothic writing.

(b) Rotunda. A style of writing having some 'Gothic' characteristics but more rounded like Roman.

(c) Jenson's Roman type that has influenced type designers down to our own day.

(d) Garamond. A French type derived from the Aldine Roman.

bottom of the mould which creates the level printing surface of the piece of type, must be absolutely flat. It would be impossible for a man with a graver to incise such a mould. The solution to the problem then is not to cut a mould but to cut a punch, in which the letter stands in relief. The punch, being made of steel, is driven into a softer metal like bronze, which produces an indentation the exact shape of the letter. It is this which becomes the mould from which types are cast.

A punch is made by a craftsman who first engraves or lightly scratches an outline of the letter on the end of a rectangular piece of steel rod. The waste metal surrounding the outline is then filed away until the letter is very precisely fashioned in high relief. Enclosed shapes such as the bowl of a capital R or a lower-case a are made with another punch called a counter-punch which is driven into the master-punch in the right position. Hence the enclosed parts of letters are now called counters.

It should be clear from this very brief explanation of punch-cutting that there is no practical reason why thicks and thins of a letter should come in a particular place as was dictated by the pen. Nor need the finials at the end of strokes be blunt or straight-edged as the pen would produce. Rounded blob-like endings to letters like lower-case c and a are just as easy to cut as the traditional pen forms. In other words, there was technically a liberation from some of the physical limitations of the pen. But aesthetically the pen and the creations of penmen provided a standard and a model on which to build a style appropriate to printing. If early printed books are finely conceived, and they are, it is due to the fact of a fine tradition of penmanship and book production at the time of the invention of printing. In Italy the influence of the Classical Renaissance made itself felt forcibly on the written and subsequently printed page. The unearthing of Roman architectural and sculptural remains was accompanied by a revival of interest in classical literature. It so happened that the text of many of these books was written in the Caroline minuscule which led to a revival of that script. A Neo-Caroline hand developed during the 15th century so that when printing was introduced into Italy by German craftsmen it was not long before the Caroline

minuscule and its derivatives began to dictate the character of printing types. The types used by the German priest-printers, Sweynheim and Pannartz, who traditionally are thought to have brought printing to Italy, were semi-gothic or rotunda, but by degrees black letter, or near black letter types were used for headlines only and were eventually abandoned, while the main body of the text of books was printed in 'white' letter, the much lighter toned letter based on humanistic script. Although black letter or textura and rotunda types were gradually supplanted by what we must now call 'roman' types, they have always been admired and from time to time revived, notably by William Morris for his Kelmscott Press at the end of the 19th century, and followed by St. John Hornby at the Ashendene Press.

The Classical Renaissance favoured the employment of humanistic types and style of layout and also the trades of publishing and bookselling, although at this time they were not separate professions. Many of the first printers were primarily scholars and they had to learn, or persuade others to learn, the trades and crafts involved in the printing, publishing and distribution of books. It was only later that typefounding, printing, publishing and so on, became separate and distinct trades.

The city of Venice, already a great centre of trade, became a great centre of printing and book production, and greatest among the printer-publishers of that time were Aldus Manutius and Nicolas Jenson.

Aldus, as he is usually called, produced many fine books both with and without illustrations. One of the most distinguished illustrated books ever published was his *Dream of Poliphilus* (*Hypnerotomachia Poliphili*). The woodcut illustrations are unsurpassed of their kind and the type is a compact, characterful, legible letter that has been recut in the 20th century for modern use. It is called Poliphilus.

In 1495, Aldus printed a tract by Cardinal Bembo in a newly made type which has so won the respect and admiration of 20th-century typographers that it has been cut as faithfully as modern technology makes possible and is available for general use under the name Bembo. For many years now in exhibitions of book production Bembo

Page from 'De Aetna' by Pietro Bembo published by Aldus Manutius in 1495. This type has been re-cut by the Monotype Corporation and called Bembo.

haec quidem certe non displicent ipsa per se : atq; etiam delectauit me non nihil poetae ingenium ; qui tam apte descripserit fluentem , et ardentem tellurem : sed tamen tu fili nimium perparce respondes ad illa , quae peto : non modo enim istud ita simpliciter cupio, ea incendia quómodo fluant ,scire abs te :sed etiam , ubi descenderint ,quam faciem capiant ; tum si perdurant éadem semper ,an aliquando immutentur, audire. BEMBVS. FIL. Geram tibi morem páter ; et ea ,quae postulas ut potero ,explicabo. Pleno iam partu (ut maturior est omnis foetus, quicunq; in Aetnae matris utero coalescit)ni su parientis expellitur ,et eiectatur, quacunq; prius rimam inuenerit , aut uiam sibi parauerit ui sua: saepe tamen exit ex cratere ,quem ipsi uidimus; nunq ex superiore; φ uel eò inscendere grauis materia non queat ;uel, quia inferius alia

has proved one of the most popular types. It is an unaffected, elegant, restrained letter that invites reading without attracting too much attention to itself. It can be seen on page 33. These two types are important not only for their beauty and utility even today, but because they are the prototypes or precursors of a major family of type forms—the Old Face family. We shall discuss the characteristics of Old Face and, in contrast, 'modern' face, shortly. Aldus also introduced the first narrow, slightly sloping letter which we call italic. It was designed and used, not for emphasis as it is today, but as a text type, the intention being to save space and produce pocket-size editions which Aldus did in large numbers. The designer and cutter for this and the Poliphilus and Bembo types was Francesco Griffo of Bologna.

Nicolas Jenson's types are, on the whole, wider and rounder than Aldus's. Serifs tend to be chunkier but the general effect of Jenson's type is open, stately and serene. Many modern types are based on Jenson's Roman, for example, Emery Walker's Dove type and Bruce Rogers's Centaur.

Books printed before 1500 are collectively known as *incunabula*, a word which literally means swaddling clothes. We now leave the period of the infancy of printing. From now on the design of printing types becomes the province of professional typefounders who had created a separate industry, supplying many printers with their types.

From the late fourteen hundreds until today the history of the design of type faces for books is largely that of subtle variations on an accepted theme. As we have already said, a number of the most popular book faces of the 20th century are virtually 15th-century Italian types and many other types familiar to modern eyes vary but little from 15th, 16th, 17th or 18th-century letters, indeed they are as close to the originals as present day methods of production and printing will permit.

In spite of the fact that the printing-press quickly took away from the scribes all the work of transcribing books, there was still a lot of work to be done for church and state by way of decrees, edicts, apostolic briefs, and other important documents particularly for the Vatican.

So instead of a decline there was an upsurge of calligraphic skill in Italy in the 16th century, especially of the italic hand called Chancery.

Another effect of the rise in the printing industry was the production of copy-books. Hitherto writing had been learned by example, by working with a teacher, but the printing of copy-books or handwriting manuals with instructions how to hold the pen, how to sit and so on, and with specimens to copy in order to acquire skill in writing made it possible for any diligent person to become a penman without the need to attend a class.

The first handwriting manual to be printed appeared in 1522. It was written by Ludovico Arrighi and was followed by G. A. Tagliente in 1524, and by G. B. Palatino in 1540. Of the writing of writing manuals there is no end. From that time on to the present, each generation has produced its copy-books, displaying with varying degrees of virtuosity whatever hands were popular in their day. The period since the Second World War has seen a deluge of writing books, most of them dealing with the Chancery Italic and its derivatives, and there has been a healthy interest in handwriting in many Primary Schools.

Books were also produced on the formation of capital letters. In some instances the authors appear to have based their work on Carolingian sources, others on Roman classical inscriptions. Two of the most famous books dealing with capital letters are *Divina Proportione* by Luca Pacioli, in 1509, and *Unterweysung der Messung* by the great German painter and engraver Albrecht Dürer, in 1525.

We have already mentioned the importance of the Aldine roman and italic, both of which influenced French designers. Perhaps the greatest of these was Claude Garamond (1480–1561) who was the first to devote himself exclusively to the designing, cutting and casting of types. His name lives on as the name of a type much used today, which is an Old Face developed from Aldine roman.

During the 16th century engraving on copper became fashionable and title-pages of books were produced from copperplates even though it meant a separate printing from the rest of the book. This was to have an influence on printing types as well as on documents and inscriptions.

Copy-books in the 17th and early 18th centuries abounded in 'copperplate' script. They were engraved with astonishing bravura and the author's self-confidence was often reflected in the wording of the titles such as *Magnum in Parvo* or *The Pen's Perfection*, *The Pen's Transcendancy*, *Pen's Triumph*, *Pen's Celerity*, *The Penman's Paradise*.

To understand the effect of this fashion on book types which were the norm of the alphabet, it is necessary to appreciate that copperplate printing is intaglio—the reverse of letterpress or relief printing. Type (and woodcuts) are printed from the raised surface, but the printing lines of a copperplate are incised, so that the printing area is below the surface. It is printed by dabbing ink into the hollows and wiping the surplus ink off the surface before applying the paper under the pressure of a heavy roller.

It is possible, indeed easy, to produce very fine hair lines and sweeping curves with a graver (burin) on a polished copper plate. When classical capital letters were engraved it was difficult to produce the gentle curve from stem to serif (which came so naturally in stone)—at least, in the small sizes required. But it was technically easy, and it was thought to look smart, if the serifs were thin—just a single stroke of the graver at right-angles to the stem, and without brackets of any sort. Such crisp, stylish engraving was seen on title-pages and maps, and it is not surprising to find a demand for something of this quality in text types. One result of the desire to produce this copperplate quality in the text was to go the whole way and engrave the text of the whole book on the plate. Imagine the tedium as well as the amazing craftsmanship required to engrave, backwards, as it would have to be for copperplate, the text of a complete book in a size about 10pt., that is, about the size of the type you are reading. But almost three hundred pages of the works of Horace were so engraved and printed, and published by John Pine in 1733. The copperplate style of lettering with swaggering flourishes invaded the churchyards and some

Page from George Shelley's 'Natural Writing', 1709. Printed from an engraved copper plate.

A B C D
a b c d e f g

(a) *Caslon's Old Face, first designed and cut during the second quarter of the 18th century and still going strong.*

A B C D
a b c d e f g

(b) *Baskerville's type, often described as transitional because of its 'modern' tendencies.*

A B C

(c) *Bodoni's fully fledged 'modern face'.*

of the finest copperplate lettering is to be seen on slate gravestones.

Before we move on to the important developments of the 18th century a few words must be said about lettering on buildings and memorials as well as books. Only the well-to-do could afford a gravestone or tomb and of those that are to be seen in England of the 16th and 17th centuries only a few, in the author's opinion, are very accomplished and many are very crude and ungainly without compensating charm. But, judging by a study of gravestones in Britain, about 1700 there was an upsurge of skill in letter-cutting, particularly on slate, and there is an abundance of stones brilliantly cut in a clear, dignified legible letter that is wholly admirable. It is not always easy to say whether these letter-cutters were influenced by printing types or whether type designers sometimes modelled their letters on those seen in their local churchyard. Lettering on buildings during this period was also good, indeed the 18th century is justly renowned for good taste in architecture and the domestic arts and crafts.

If most of the major improvements in the form of letters for printing up to this time had been continental, in the 18th century England produced types which were to influence continental designers in the establishment of the style called 'modern' face.

The first man to make his mark was William Caslon, an engraver of gun barrels, who produced letter stamps for bookbinders and eventually turned typefounder. Between 1720 and 1726 he cut his famous Old Face series which is as good and usable today as it was two hundred years ago and is very English in spite of Dutch precedents.

About the middle of the century a remarkable character named John Baskerville, who had been among other things a writing-master and a manufacturer of lacquered goods, in middle age took up printing and made a major contribution to type design and book production. His type is called transitional because it has some of the characteristics of Old Face such as the bracketed serifs, but it has some of the characteristics of modern face such as the vertical stress in the curved letters. It is a round, wide-set letter that is still very popular today.

Because Baskerville wanted to get something of the

sharpness in his printing that was prevalent in copper-plate he experimented with paper to overcome the tendency for the shapes of letters to be blurred when printed. All printing was by hand, on damp hand-made paper which had the effect of thickening the printed image. Baskerville thought up the idea of pressing his sheets of paper between hot plates to produce a smooth surface so that he could make the most of his carefully designed letters.

Baskerville was a book-typographer as well as a type-designer and printer and he rejected ornament of all kind, believing that shapely roman letters carefully spaced were decorative enough.

This austerity of layout and a tendency to 'modern' in style of letter form was carried a stage further by Bodoni in Italy. By 1780 the style we know as modern face was fully established.

Until the late 18th century types were produced mainly for books—for text or display on title-pages. Lettering on buildings, whether ecclesiastical, municipal or commercial, was small in quantity and the style was conditioned by book and tombstone typography. But with the expansion of advertising fostered by the increase in newspapers and magazines made possible by steam printing and machine-made paper, types were designed for use on posters and handbills that were bold and rumbustious, that spoke with the voice of the market-place rather than the cloister.

Without the restraining hand of the churchman or the scholar it became possible to take liberties with letters that would have been unthinkable in previous centuries.

Typefounders, still one of the chief sources of letter design, produced fat faces, thin faces, plain faces, fancy faces. In the 19th century there was a general liberation from the restraining influence of classical Roman lettering which was not treated as sacred, as if any sort of modification was a defilement. Letters were regarded as legitimate fields for fantasy. People, animals, trees—anything—were persuaded, cajoled, pushed, pressed, forced into the shape of letters of the alphabet if the objects were in some way appropriate to the text. To those who do not like the alphabet to be tampered with, the Victorian era

was one of decadence. To those who put creativity before convention it was a period of great vitality.

Text types and book-typography during most of the 19th century is not, in general, to our taste. It was abhorred by William Morris who in the 'nineties founded his Kelmscott Press in order to restore, as he thought, the course of book design into its proper channel. When Morris first became interested in book production he could not find a commercial printer (and there were no others) with a good enough type and high enough standards of format and press work to satisfy his fastidious taste. He studied, and was rich enough to buy, medieval manuscripts and books of the *incunabula* period especially those in semi-gothic or rotunda types. He admired the decorative borders of Ratdolt, another famous printer of the 15th century, and his own designs reflect this enthusiasm. The 15th-century book was to him the ideal book, or so it would seem, as he modelled his types and the format of his books on that period, though the final result would no doubt seem strange to a 15th-century printer were it possible for him to see Morris's ornamental volumes. Morris's types seem to me to have little relevance today, but his principles and his spirit are eternal.

The printer who advised Morris on the setting up of his press, Emery Walker, himself went into partnership with a flamboyant character named T. J. Cobden-Sanderson, to found the Doves Press. The special type they designed, the Doves type, was modelled on Jenson's Roman and was a very good type indeed, very appropriate for the Bible which is the monumental achievement of the press. But,

Diagram and description of the characteristics of 'Old Face' and 'Modern Face'.

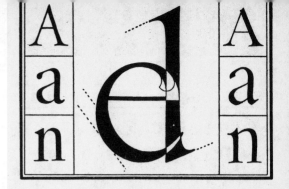

1. Point of maximum stress at an angle.
2. Gradual transition from thick to thin strokes.
3. Little contrast between thick and thin strokes (there are exceptions).
4. Serifs bracketed.
5. Serifs of lower-case letters like d, b, n, m, etc., at an angle (see diagram).

Good Old Face types are Bembo, Caslon Old Face, Garamond, Plantin.

1. Point of maximum stress vertical.
2. Abrupt transition from thick to thin strokes.
3. Strong contrast between thick and thin strokes (hairlines).
4. Serifs usually (but not always) unbracketed.
5. Serifs of lower-case letters like d, b, l, etc., horizontal.

Good Modern Face types are Bodoni, Walbaum, Bell, Scotch Roman.

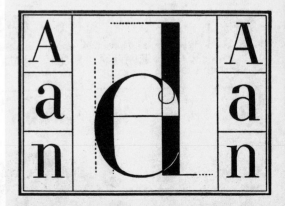

alas, the type was imposed on the bed of the Thames by Cobden-Sanderson who threw it over Hammersmith Bridge rather than relinquish it to Emery Walker after the dissolution of their partnership.

The Doves type and Doves austere format without any decoration—not even rules—have some relevance today. Their disciplined approach to the whole concept of typography has affinities with our own approach though our technical resources are so much greater and we aim at a different public.

William Morris was at the inception of the Arts and

Crafts Movement with its insistence on the best materials, fine craftsmanship, utter sincerity and 'joy in the making'. It was a philosophy of art and design which pervaded everything. It led to the founding of the Central School of Arts and Crafts in London under W. R. Lethaby. It was dedicated to principles that anticipated and ante-dated the Bauhaus founded by Walter Gropius in 1919.

In that movement was Edward Johnston, a great individualist who devoted his life with persistence and little financial profit to the study, practice and teaching of calligraphy. His book *Writing and Illuminating, and Lettering* is perhaps one of the most influential books on lettering ever published. Through this book, and the students he trained while teaching at the Royal College of Art and the Central School, Johnston helped to bring about a 20th-century renaissance of lettering. In many ways he was a medievalist, as were so many in the Arts and Crafts Movement, and he made a penetrating study of old manuscripts on which he based his style and pre-cepts; but it was Johnston who designed the uncom-promisingly functional sans serif letter for the London Underground Railway which led the way to the present vogue for 'sans' types.

If in Roman times the inscriptional capital was the norm, and in medieval times the manuscript minuscule was the model and the style-forming influence in lettering, in the 20th century printing types certainly constitute the force which tends to mould alphabetic taste. Everybody sees millions of printed letters, many of them fine in form; only a few individuals, like employees in the manuscript department of museums, see enough calligraphy for it to be much of an influence, and letters cut in stone play but a small part in most people's lives. But the place of classical, inscriptional lettering on buildings has been taken by letters in a variety of materials from plastic to bronze and from stainless steel to neon tubes. It is im-

(a) A book-mark, woven in silk with an ornamental alphabet as decoration. Victorian.

(b) A few types from Wood's Typographic Advertiser 1864.

Two-line Great Primer. 2/3 the set.

Cr͏ L Mr. D͏

Double Pica Clarendon. 15 lbs. 14/ the lot.

Summer is coming SUNSHINE.

Two-line Pica Shaded Ornamented. 5 lbs. 7/5 the lot.

JUDGE MERTON

Two-line English Extended Clarendon. 30 lbs. 25/ the lot.

Householder EXAMINE

Two-line Double Pica Ornamented. 8 lbs. 12/ the lot.

STEAM

Four-line Pica Elzevir Antique. 12 lbs. 13/6 the lot.

Manipulation 16

Five-line Condensed Clarendon. 25 lbs. 19/ the lot.

ROME,

(a) *A charming typographic 'floral tribute'.*

226

PEERESSES' GALLERY.

Funeral of the Late
Field Marshal The Duke of Wellington, K.G.
Admit a Lady
to S.t Paul's Cathedral.

Norfolk.
Earl Marshal.

(b) *Dignity and restraint are expressed in this card for the Duke of Wellington's funeral. Copperplate script surrounded by a Greek fret border.*

EVENING PRAYER.

Blessed Lord, who hast safely brought me to the close of this day; accept my humble praise for this and all other mercies conferred upon me. Pardon the sins I have committed against thee this day, and preserve me this night from all evil, for Jesus Christ's sake. Amen.

A B C D E
F G H I J K
L M N O P
Q R S T U
V W X Y Z
a b c d e f g h
i j k l m n o p
q r s t u v w x
y z æ œ &
fi ff fl ffi ffl

A B C D E
F G H I J K
L M N O P
Q R S T U
V W X Y Z
a b c d e f g h
i j k l m n o p
q r s t u v w
x y z æ œ &
fi ff fl ffi ffl

(c) *These cards were mounted on a thin wooden board like a battledore to be held in the hand for children to learn the alphabet.*

possible to escape these. It would be surprising if their presence did not have some influence on people's taste and must therefore be taken into account even in such a short sketch of the story of the alphabet as this. Names on shop fronts are in a bewildering variety of styles. At one end of the scale there are the architect controlled, carefully integrated letters by designers who specialize in lettering. Here the name of the business is made to harmonize with the building and its neighbours. At the other end of the scale are the brash, vulgar, tasteless forms where large size is thought to be the only criterion of legibility, where the proprietor has had his signature enlarged and painted or cast in metal. Some very famous firms have as their trade-mark what was originally the founder's handwriting, but it has been copied and re-copied in such a motley of materials that the forms are so changed that only the faintest semblance of the cursive signature remains.

40

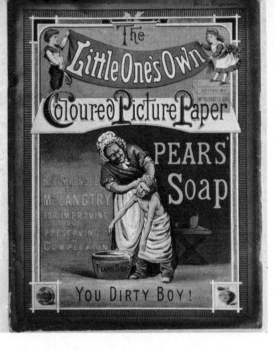

Another very public kind of lettering is that on railway and bus stations, docks and airports. Frequently in the past these were inconsistent, illegible, scrappy; often designed and placed with crass disregard of architectural amenity and even of passenger needs. But new airports are setting a standard of functional and aesthetic understanding that is fortunately spreading. The new universities are breaking away from a stodgy traditionalism which was often more of a clinging to safe convention than an understanding of the main stream of tradition. Many blocks of offices and department stores are now pleasingly and functionally signposted and labelled, but many municipal buildings are still defaced with ill-lettered, badly placed and spaced signs. Some colleges, even colleges of art, are going up all over the country with little thought given to the form and function of lettering and the needs of both occupants and visitors. Names and numbers, scribbled or typed, are stuck on doors with adhesive tape and bear no relation to the rest of the decor, nor is there any consistency or hierarchy of style that enables the visitor readily to find the room he wants; even a resident in a large college is as much a 'visitor' in an unfamiliar part of the college as a stranger.

Finally, there is another use of lettering which has an impact on the public, namely, traffic signs. As we said at the beginning, in the design of signs for traffic and the traveller we are, for some purposes, back, so to speak, to the origins of the alphabet, back to designing signs and symbols to convey an immediate message to command, to warn, to guide, to advise.

Letters on buildings and in streets may be painted on wood, metal, brick, glass, stone, concrete; they may be cast in metal, plastic, pottery, cement; they may be cut, engraved, forged in metal or plastic, and all may be illuminated. Illumination may be from within or without. All these things tend to modify the shapes of the alphabet

(a) Cover of a children's picture paper which also contains an advertisement. The style of lettering is typical of the end of the 19th and beginning of the 20th century.

(b) Art Nouveau when it was really new.

GEWÖHNLICH
GLAUBT DER
MENSCH,
WENN ER
NUR WORTE
HÖRT, ES
MÜSSE SICH
DABEI DOCH
AUCH WAS
DENKEN
LASSEN GOETHE

Four examples of recent hand lettering from Germany. The Germans have a reputation for calligraphic fecundity which seems to have been stimulated during the rebuilding of their country since the war.

but the chief restraining influence is still the roman letter (but not necessarily the classical, inscriptional letter) and mainly through type faces. Sometimes the influence is too strong and we see letter forms designed for books enlarged and made from alien materials and used without proper adaptation to the intended purpose.

If, then, we regard printing types as the main source of inspiration for letter forms we find that types themselves are in an enormous variety of styles. Book types are in the main 'roman' tradition and are only minutely different from the 15th century. Display types, on the other hand, reflect practically every phase of fashion and though most have a short life some are sufficiently good to be revived again and again.

It is always difficult to define the trends of the age in which one lives and even more difficult to be sure which are likely to survive and become part of the tradition which will help form the style of the next generation, but one might say there are two important trends in lettering and typography today. There is the austere, ascetic tradition that favours the sans serif letter, eschews ornament, has a liking for large areas of space and small sizes of type, is inclined to stick to one type family only and is severely functional in its philosophy. Is this the 'true' 20th-century style? Is the sans serif letter the symbol of the 20th century, as has been suggested, even though the sans serif letter has been used since the early 19th century,

42

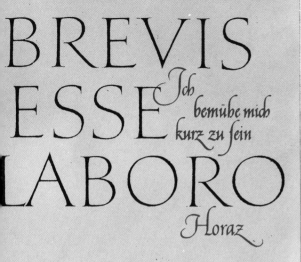

BREVIS
ESSE *Ich bemühe mich kurz zu sein*
LABORO
Horaz

Manchmal will unser Licht erlöschen und wird dann durch ein Erlebnis mit einem Menschen wieder neu entfacht. So hat jeder von uns mit tiefem Dank derer zu gedenken, die Flammen in ihm entzündet haben.

and even though the earliest Greek and Latin lettering had no serifs? Future historians may decide, but we can say here and now that this tradition is a healthy one, that sans serif is here to stay, that it has acquired status against the barrage of disapproval by traditionalists with Renaissance tastes. If there is a danger, it is that the sans serif may become 'respectable' and be used just as tastelessly as have traditional serifed letters. In the meantime, at its best, this clean functional style that was propagated with

near-religious fervour by a group of designers in Switzerland after the Second World War and has won fanatical devotees all over the world, has produced some of the most interesting typographic design of this century.

Alongside this sharply contrasting philosophy there has been a school of thought in reaction from austerity, that has found nourishment for its ideas in Art Nouveau and encouraged decoration to the point of flamboyance even in lettering. To the practitioners of the school the tradi-

tional roman norm is subservient to the nature of the occasion. If the occasion is frivolous—then the letters may be frivolous. Instant legibility is not always paramount. If that is so, why not let the imagination have free rein; why not let letters of the alphabet be the basis of an abstract fantasy. After all, are not the letters of the alphabet in themselves abstract shapes having beauty in their own right apart from the ideas they may express, or the emotions they may evoke?

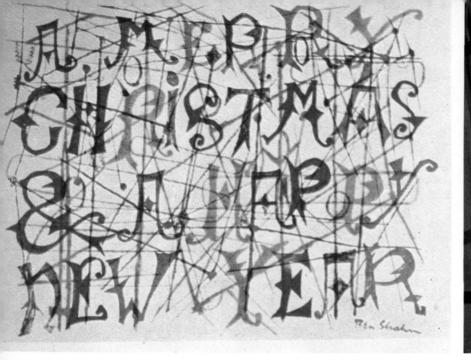

(a) Letters appropriately fantastic and joyous for a Christmas Card by Ben Shahn.
(b) Suitably dignified sign outside show rooms.
(c) Highly polished metal letters for a clothing shop.

OPPOSITE

(a) Simple, easily legible letters for signs on the new British motorways.
(b) An old sign post which has charm while still performing its proper function in a rural setting. The letters are painted on wood.
(c) Derbyshire cast iron mile post. Sturdy and legible.
(d) Parisian bus-stop.
(e) Street sign in Paris.

44

London Colchester A12
Stratford St. Mary
Dedham
B 1029

•DORSET•
6^d HANDLEY
995172

WOODCUTTS 1½
B CRANBORNE 5½
RINGWOOD 14
SALISBURY 13½
TOLLARD ROYAL 3½
SHAFTESBURY 11¼
E
30

LONDON
142 MILES
DERBY
16 MILES
BENTLEY PARISH
BUXTON
17 MILES

CAMBRONNE

13^e ARR^t
BOULEVARD
AUGUSTE BLANQUI

(a) Book jackets.
(b) Metal lettering outside a swimming bath.
(c) Metal letters over a shop.
(d) Illuminated lettering over a café.

OPPOSITE
(a) Letters in concrete outside a University.
(b) A students' project cut in expanded polystyrene.
(c) Pierced and engraved metal on a door in a Paris typefoundry.
(d) Letters engraved on a glass goblet.

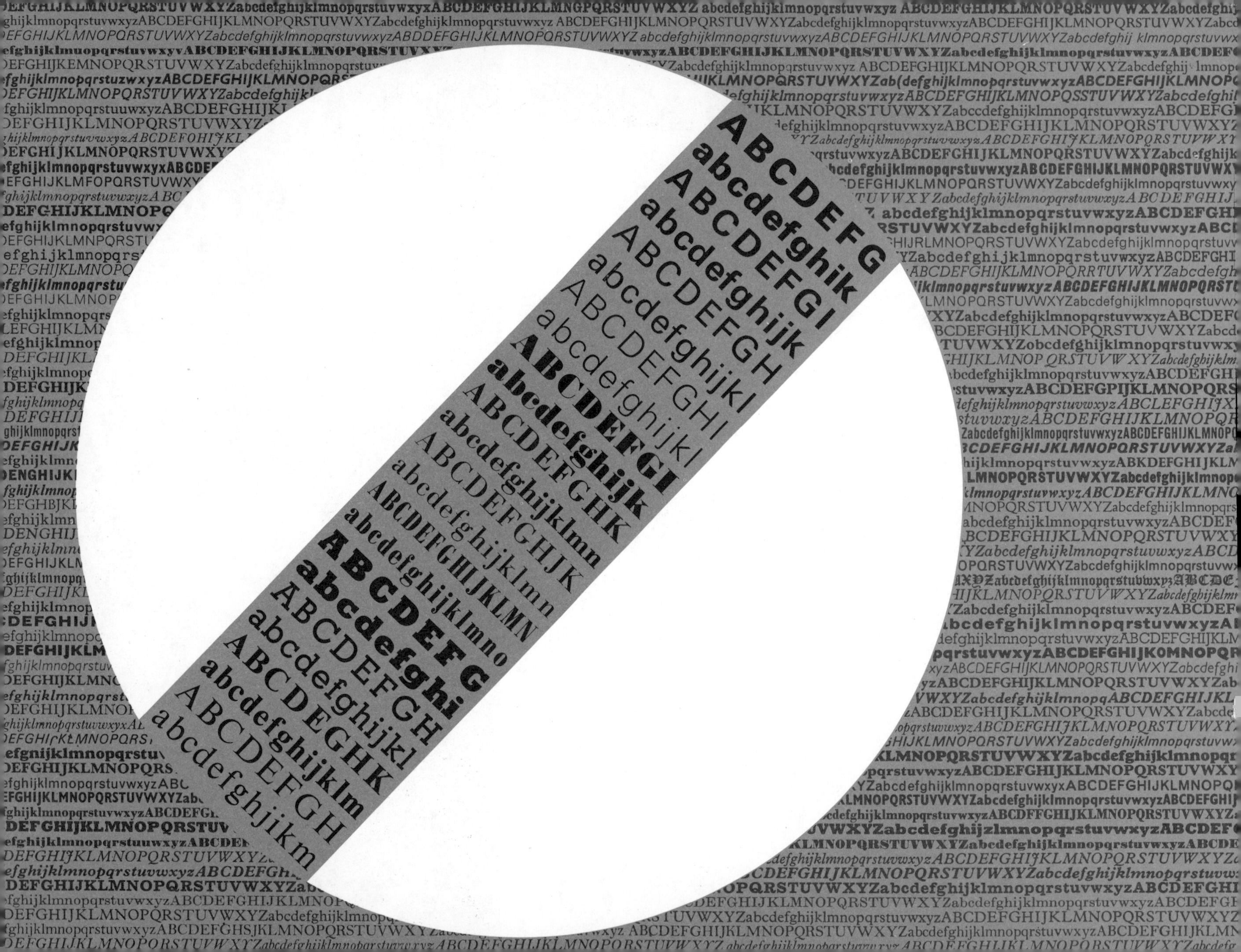

ABCDEFG
abcdefghik
ABCDEFGI
abcdefghijk
ABCDEFGH
abcdefghijkl
ABCDEFGHI
abcdefghijkl
ABCDEFGI
abcdefghijk
ABCDEFGHK
abcdefghijklmn
ABCDEFGHJK
abcdefghijklmn
ABCDEFGHIJKLMN
abcdefghijklmno
ABCDEFG
abcdefghi
ABCDEFGH
abcdefghijkl
ABCDEGHK
abcdefghijklm
ABCDEFGH
abcdefghijkm